How to be  a Tween Superstar!

Inspiring stories of pre-teen kids changing the world with courage, creativity, determination, optimism, and compassion.

TWEEN SUCCESS

ISBN: 978-1-915833-05-1

Disclaimer: The information in this book is general and designed to be for information only. It is a work of creative nonfiction designed to inspire the next generation of leaders, activists, and changemakers. While every effort has been made to ensure it is wholly accurate, it is not intended to be an encyclopedia of the lives of the tweens included in the book.

This book belongs to:

_____

_____

SOMETHING
FOR YOU

Get your <u>FREE</u> Printable Workbook!

 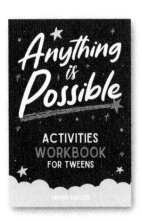

To download your free workbook

SCAN
HERE

Table of Contents

Be Inspired!

Imagine a world where young kids are inspiring, achieving, and literally changing our world! They are the changemakers, sports stars, and heroes of our time. They are fighting for justice and raising money for those in need. They are conquering mountains and swimming oceans.

YOU DON'T NEED TO IMAGINE IT BECAUSE THIS WORLD ALREADY EXISTS! AND YOU'RE IN IT!

This book is an inspiring collection of stories about extraordinary young people who have achieved incredible things in their short lives.

Some of them you may already know about, and others you'll hear about for the first time. But each of them has done something incredible to make the world better in some way, shape, or form.

FROM CHILD ACTIVISTS FIGHTING INJUSTICE TO INVENTORS AND ENTREPRENEURS, THIS BOOK WILL HAVE YOU IN AWE OF THE POWER AND TENACITY OF YOUNG PEOPLE.

Take Joshua Williams, for example. When he was just four years old, Joshua set up his own foundation to help feed underprivileged families across the US. Fast forward 16 years and his organization's impact has been felt worldwide. His foundation has served almost five million meals and has raised millions of dollars.

Or how about Marley Dias? When she was 11 years old, Marley started her movement to promote diversity in children's literature. Within a year of launching her campaign, she had reached her goal of collecting 1,000 books with black female protagonists and donated them to underprivileged schools.

You'll also meet:
- A young athlete who became the youngest Olympic medal winner in history.
- A 12-year-old girl whose invention saved lives.
- A brave tween who is leading the fight against climate change.
- A young boy who climbed Mount Everest.

Although each story is unique, you'll find that many of the featured individuals have similar qualities and skills.

That's because it takes determination, courage, and dedication to succeed, whether it's conquering a mountain or starting a movement.

You'll learn about these qualities and how to apply them in your own life to become the next generation of activists, sports stars, and heroes.

At the end of each chapter, you'll find a series of activities designed to help you develop the skills and qualities necessary for success.

There's a world of possibilities out there for young people who have dreams and won't take no for an answer. This book is here to inspire you and show you that anything is possible with hard work and dedication.

Get ready to be inspired by some of the most incredible young people from around the world!

Let's dive in and explore just how extraordinary kids can be!

SOME PEOPLE WANT it TO HAPPEN, SOME WISH it WOULD HAPPEN, OTHERS MAKE it HAPPEN.

- Michael Jordan

COURAGE

OVERCOMING FEAR AND
TAKING ACTION

It's better to be
a **LiON** for a day
than a **SHEEP**
 all your life.

- Elizabeth Kenny

Have you ever wanted to do something big but felt scared? Perhaps you had an idea that could make a positive difference in the world but were afraid of what other people might think. Or maybe you wanted to try something new, like learning a foreign language or taking up a sport but were worried about failing.

No matter what you want to do, courage is essential for achieving success in life.

But what exactly is courage?

Courage means doing difficult and sometimes even scary things and having the strength to carry on regardless of what people think or say. It's pushing through adversity and staying motivated despite any external influences that may make you doubt yourself.

Courage is like a muscle — the more you use it, the stronger it becomes. By accomplishing complex tasks and striving to do what's right, your courage will grow until you can take on much bigger challenges. As with physical exercise, using your courage builds strength and resilience so that when the going gets tough, you'll be ready to take it on.

Courage allows us to stand up for what we believe in and make a positive difference in the world. It is the driving force behind creating meaningful change in our communities and beyond.

This chapter will explore the stories of incredible young people who have shown immense courage. We'll learn how their courage helped them achieve their goals, fight for justice, and inspire others. We will also consider how courage can help us face our own fears and take risks in life.

By the end of this chapter, you'll have a greater understanding of why courage is an important quality to cultivate in order to succeed!

Sam Berns

AMERICAN PROGERIA ACTIVIST

Sam Berns raised awareness and funds for Progeria research, inspired millions of people with his TED Talk, and left a lasting legacy of hope and happiness.

You can't pick the hand you're dealt in life, but you can choose how to play the cards.

Sam Berns was just like any other kid of his age. He loved music, scouting, and playing in his high school band with his friends. But there was one big difference between Sam and other kids his age: Sam had progeria.

Progeria is a rare condition that causes children to age much faster than usual. It is a genetic disease, and most kids with progeria die before age 20. Sam was diagnosed with progeria when he was just two years old, and by the time he was a teenager, he looked like an elderly man.

Despite the challenges of living with progeria, Sam refused to let the disease define him. He was determined to live a normal life and make a difference in the world — and he did just that.

Sam became an ambassador for the Progeria Research Foundation, working to raise awareness and funds for research into the disease. He also appeared on TV shows and gave speeches to help educate people about progeria.

Sam's TED Talk, "My Philosophy for a Happy Life," has been viewed over 50 million times and inspired others to live their best lives. In it, he shares his three simple principles for happiness:

MAKE THE BEST OF WHAT YOU CAN DO, SURROUND YOURSELF WITH PEOPLE YOU LOVE, AND FIND SOMETHING TO LOOK FORWARD TO.

Sadly, Sam passed away in 2014 at the age of 17. But his legacy of hope and happiness lives on. His story continues to inspire people worldwide, proving that anyone can make a difference — no matter how young they are.

Tom Gregory

ENGLISH SWIMMER

Tom Gregory is an inspiring swimmer who became the youngest person ever to successfully complete a solo swim of the English Channel.

Imagine breaking a world record at just 11 years of age. Not just any record—the youngest person in the world to swim across the English Channel!

In 1988, before today's tweens were born, Tom Gregory did just that.

HE WAS ONLY 11 YEARS OLD WHEN HE SWAM THE ENGLISH CHANNEL, SETTING A WORLD RECORD THAT WILL LIKELY NEVER BE BROKEN.

The English Channel is a stretch of water that separates England from France. It's about 22 miles (35 kilometers) wide, is one of the busiest shipping lanes in the world, and is usually very cold, ranging from 45 °F (7 °C) in February to 61 °F (16 °C) in September.

But while Tom's exceptional swimming skills made him famous, he didn't get there without first having to endure great pain and sacrifice.

When Tom was six years old, he and his sister joined Coach John Bullet's swimming club in Southeast London. John was known for his ability to get his young swimmers to do incredible things. In 1979, he had successfully trained 12-year-old Marcus Hooper to swim the Channel. He was the youngest person to do so until John guided Tom towards achieving the same feat two years later.

Tom and his coach were fully aware of the dangers of swimming the Channel. Just nine days before his attempt, a 20-year-old woman from Brazil had died of hypothermia while attempting to do it. Hypothermia is when your body loses heat faster than it can produce it, and it's a genuine danger in the cold waters of the English Channel.

While Tom's parents were apprehensive about their young boy trying to swim so far after the tragic death, Tom was not deterred. He believed in himself and his coach's plan. He was determined to achieve something no one his age had ever done — swim the English Channel.

Before he could embark on his challenge, Tom had to condition his body to withstand the extreme conditions of the channel.

Starting in Christmas 1987, a year before his cross-channel attempt, Tom quit using hot water. Instead, he took cold showers and baths to prepare him for the cold of the channel. Then, starting in the spring of 1988, he slept every night with the window open and only one sheet to cover him.

He also pushed himself to the limit physically with a rigorous training regime that included long-distance open-water training swims. For this purpose, Tom's coach chose Lake Windermere, one of England's largest and deepest lakes. The lake offered Tom a safe place to practice swimming long distances and develop his endurance and strength.

When it was finally time for Tom to take on his challenge, he was ready. With his coach's help and strong determination, Tom successfully completed the swim in under 12 hours. Later, he wrote an award-winning book about his experience, "A Boy in the Water," in which he talks in detail about the mental toll of taking on such a vast physical challenge. According to his account, during the 12 hours of swimming, Tom was reduced to tears, experienced hallucinations, and became so exhausted that he struggled to remain conscious.

Despite his struggles, Tom does not regret swimming the channel and has fond memories of his coach John. The pair had discussed attempting other long-distance swimming challenges, but sadly John passed away shortly after Tom's record-breaking swim. According to Tom, it was "like losing a father."

After losing John, Tom never swam long distances again. He wrote his book and went on to serve in the military.

Tom's record will likely never be broken. A decade after Tom's successful attempt, the Channel Swimming Association banned anyone younger than 16 from attempting to swim across the channel.

While his achievements may seem a bit dangerous by today's standards, Tom's incredible story proves that anything is possible with dedication, courage, and determination.

Jaylen Arnold

AMERICAN ANTI-BULLYING CAMPAIGNER

Jaylen Arnold is an inspiring anti-bullying campaigner who has used his story and platform to help countless people around the world stand up against bullying.

Being bullied is not a pleasant experience, and it can be tough to cope with. Unfortunately, it's an all-too-common occurrence for many kids in schools and communities worldwide.

But bullies never win! Jaylen Arnold, a boy from Florida, proves precisely this. Despite his struggles with bullying, Jaylen decided to take action and make a difference. He founded his own charity, "Jaylen's Challenge Foundation," which is dedicated to spreading positivity by engaging kids and teens in anti-bullying campaigns.

Jaylen's struggles with bullying started when he was just a young boy. When he was three, Jaylen was diagnosed with Tourette syndrome. Tourette's is a neurological disorder that triggers physical and verbal tics. Because of this, Jaylen often found himself the target of bullies. A few years later, when

Jaylen was eight, he was also diagnosed with Asperger's syndrome, a form of autism.

Rather than letting his difficulties define him, Jaylen decided to use them to inspire others dealing with similar issues. He set up his foundation to spread the message of anti-bullying and raise awareness of this critical issue. Since then, Jaylen has spoken at hundreds of schools to thousands of children. He has met film stars and celebrities in his mission to create a better world. He has become an inspiration for other young kids who are facing similar struggles.

JAYLEN'S RESILIENCE, COURAGE, AND DETERMINATION HAVE HELPED HIM SHAPE THE WORLD FOR THE BETTER.

He is a living example of how one person can make a huge difference in society, regardless of age or circumstance. Jaylen's actions show that bullying will never win and that it is possible to rise above anything and create positive change. He has inspired many people with his incredible story and continues to positively impact the world.

Anoyara Khatun

INDIAN CHILDREN'S RIGHTS ACTIVIST

Anoyara Khatun has dedicated her life to rescuing hundreds of trafficked children and fighting for the rights of all young people.

Children are the future and need plenty of love, care, protection, and education to reach their full potential. But sadly, not all kids have access to these fundamental rights. In some countries, children are forced into labor or other forms of exploitation. This is called child trafficking, and it's a huge global problem, affecting an estimated four million children globally.

Anoyara Khatun knows what it's like to be a victim of child trafficking. Born into poverty in West Bengal, India, she lost her father when she was very young and was taken to Delhi, where she was forced to cook and clean from the age of 12.

After a few months, Anoyara escaped, returning to her home village, Choto Asgara. But she soon discovered that many other children were being forced into labor. Some girls were even forced to marry at a young age.

Anoyara was determined to improve life for children in her own village and others like hers. She discovered an organization called "Save the Children," which taught her that children have rights. According to the law in India, all children have the right to be protected from neglect, exploitation, and abuse.

Anoyara wanted to ensure all children had the rights they were supposed to enjoy under the law. She became a children's rights advocate and formed a network of children's groups in villages around West Bengal. The groups worked together with her to bring an end to child trafficking, child labor, and child marriages.

Now, 14 years later, Anoyara and her fellow activists have achieved some incredible things. They have stopped more than 50 child marriages, rescued more than 80 children from forced labor, and prevented the trafficking of more than 200 children.

As a result of these efforts, more than 400 children have been placed back into primary education.

Due to her work to help children, Anoyara was given the Nari Shakti Puraskar Award by Indian President Pranab Mukherjee, the highest honor awarded to Indian women. She was nominated for the International Children's Peace Prize and was invited to speak at the United Nations General Assembly.

Now 26 years old, Anoyara still works to make life better for the children of India. Thanks to the journey she embarked on as a tween, many young girls and boys now have the opportunity to go to school and lead an everyday life. Anoyara continues to inspire, proving that kids are never too young to make a difference.

Jazz Jennings

AMERICAN LGBTQ+ ACTIVIST, YOUTUBER, & AUTHOR

Through her activism and public storytelling, Jazz Jennings has opened the door to greater acceptance and understanding of transgender people worldwide.

Jazz Jennings is an LGBTQ+ activist, YouTuber, television personality, author, and spokesmodel. She was born male, but she was already questioning her identity by age two. Jazz was diagnosed with gender dysphoria, also known as gender identity disorder. This is when a person experiences discomfort or distress because there's a mismatch between their biological sex and their gender identity.

Gender identity disorder amongst kids is not that common, with only 1 in 30,000 children diagnosed with it. As a result, it can sometimes be hard for adults to accept their children are transgender. But Jazz's parents were very supportive. From a young age, Jazz dressed as a girl at home while still presenting as a boy to the outside world.

However, in 2007 at age six, Jazz and her family decided to go public with her story on the TV show "20/20." This made her one of the youngest people to come out as transgender. It was incredibly courageous. Back then, there wasn't nearly as much awareness or acceptance of transgender people as there is today. But Jazz hoped that, by sharing her story, she could help other kids like her who were struggling with their identity.

Since then, Jazz has become a powerful voice for the transgender community. In 2014, she starred in her own reality show, "I Am Jazz," which followed her everyday life. The show was groundbreaking, giving people a rare insight into what it's like to be a transgender teenager.

Jazz has also written two books, "Being Jazz: My Life as a (Transgender) Teen" and "I Am Jazz." These books help to educate people about what it means to be transgender, and they've helped to make Jazz one of the most famous teenage activists in the world.

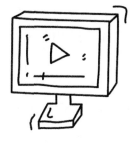

In 2014, Jazz was named one of Time magazine's "25 Most Influential Teens." She has appeared on numerous TV shows and met with President Barack Obama to discuss transgender rights. This shows the impact Jazz has had at such a young age.

JAZZ HAS SINGLEHANDEDLY CREATED A POWERFUL PLATFORM THAT IS HELPING TO CHANGE THE WAY SOCIETY VIEWS AND TREATS TRANSGENDER PEOPLE.

Iqbal Masih

PAKISTANI CHILD LABOR ACTIVIST

Iqbal Masih's bravery and activism helped raise awareness of the injustice of bonded labor and improved the rights of child laborers.

Can you remember what you were doing when you were four years old? Perhaps you remember your birthday or your first day at school?

Sadly, Iqbal Masih had none of those experiences. At the tender age of four, he started working in Pakistan's carpet weaving industry.

Iqbal was born into a poor family in Pakistan. When he was four years old, he was sold into slavery. His mom had borrowed money from a loan shark, and when she couldn't repay the debt, she had no choice but to give her son up as collateral.

Iqbal became a bonded laborer. Bonded labor is a form of slavery where people are forced to work against their will and often receive no pay.

Iqbal was put to work in a carpet factory, where he had to knot carpets for 12 hours a day. The conditions were terrible and the factory owners often beat him. He was given little food and earned less than five cents a day. His plight was hopeless. He was just a child, but he was treated like a piece of property. Without the money to pay off the debt, he would be stuck in the factory forever.

But Iqbal was a fighter. He refused to accept his situation and planned to escape. After five long years working in the factory, he finally made his break for freedom.

But his freedom was short-lived. Instead of prosecuting the owners of the factory for their harsh treatment of Iqbal and the other workers, the police returned him to the very people who had enslaved him.

Iqbal had tasted freedom, albeit briefly, and he was not going to give up. When Iqbal was 10 years old, he finally escaped the factory. He was helped by Ehsan Ullah Khan, who founded an organization called the Bonded Labour Liberation Front (BLLF).

The BLLF helped Iqbal get an education and speak out against child labor. Iqbal was free, but he had seen firsthand the horrific conditions in which many other children like him were forced to work. He was determined to do something about it.

So, Iqbal started touring Pakistan, giving speeches about his experiences and raising awareness about bonded labor. He also testified against factory owners in court, which led to several of them being jailed.

His work earned him death threats from the "carpet mafia," who relied on cheap child labor to produce carpets. But Iqbal was not afraid. He continued to speak out.

"Bonded labor is slavery, and I will fight it until the last breath in my body," he said.

Iqbal's activism eventually caught the attention of the international media, and he became a well-known child rights activist.

But Iqbal's work made him a target, and in 1995, when he was just 12 years old, he was shot and killed by an unknown assailant. His murder remains unsolved.

Iqbal's story is one of tragedy, courage, and hope. He faced injustice and cruelty from a young age. Still, he never gave up fighting for what he believed in. By harnessing his own experiences, he was able to help bring about change for other child laborers.

IQBAL IS A HERO AND HIS LEGACY CONTINUES TO INSPIRE OTHERS TO STAND UP FOR WHAT IS RIGHT.

Activity - Courage Collage

Sometimes, you have to find the courage to believe in yourself and take that first step toward making your dreams come true. Here's a fun activity for you to do: Make a courage collage.

A courage collage is a collection of images and words that remind you of courage and inspire you to keep going. It will help motivate and encourage you when times get tough and serve as a daily reminder that you have what it takes!

To make your courage collage:
- Get some paper and magazines/newspapers, or search for images online.
- Look for words, symbols, and images that represent courage to you.
- Cut out or draw the words and images and stick them onto your paper.
- Add any other details that represent courage (e.g., quotes, colors, etc.).
- Hang your collage where you can see it. This could be on the wall in your bedroom or kitchen.

This activity will help you to stay inspired, take action, and make a difference in the world! We hope it serves as a reminder that you can achieve anything you want.

Courage Collage

Add drawings, quotes or write about people
you admire or who motivate you.

COURAGE is

Standing up to
bullies

My
Hero

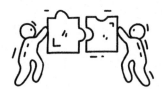

CREATIVITY

USING IMAGINATION TO CHANGE THE WORLD

CREATIVITY

IS SEEING

what others see and

THINKING

what no one else

EVER THOUGHT.

- Albert Einstein

Have you ever noticed how different kids can be?

Some like to draw, others to build, and others to dance or sing. This is because every child is creative in their own unique way.

Sometimes people confuse creativity and art, but they are two different things. Art is a form of expression, while creativity is a way of thinking. Creativity can be found in every aspect of life, from science and engineering to problem-solving and business.

CREATIVITY IS ABOUT LOOKING AT THINGS DIFFERENTLY AND COMING UP WITH ORIGINAL SOLUTIONS.

For instance, let's say you're having a tough time getting the hang of a new math concept. You could try using your creativity to develop a different approach to understanding it, such as finding examples in everyday life or creating musical rhythms.

In this chapter, we will meet some incredible tweens who demonstrate how creativity can be an invaluable asset for success. We'll learn how these young people have used their creativity to do incredible things and make a positive difference in their communities and beyond.

By the end of this chapter, you will better understand why creativity is essential for success and how to use it to your advantage!

Clara Ma

AMERICAN STUDENT: NAMED THE MARS ROVER "CURIOSITY"

Clara Ma named the Mars Science Laboratory rover "Curiosity," helping to explore a new planet and inspiring young people to pursue their dreams.

Imagine seeing your name travel into space, thousands of miles from Earth on a planet nobody has ever set foot on. That's precisely what happened to Clara Ma, a 12-year-old student from Kansas, USA.

In 2009, as a sixth-grade student, Clara entered a NASA competition to name the new Mars Science Laboratory rover. Her winning entry was "Curiosity." Why Curiosity? Let's have Clara explain in her own words:

"CURIOSITY IS AN EVERLASTING FLAME THAT BURNS IN EVERYONE'S MIND. IT MAKES ME GET OUT OF BED IN THE MORNING AND WONDER WHAT SURPRISES LIFE WILL THROW AT ME THAT DAY. CURIOSITY IS SUCH A POWERFUL FORCE. WITHOUT IT, WE WOULDN'T BE WHO WE ARE TODAY."

Clara's essay was chosen from among 9,000 entries from students across America. As part of her prize, she visited NASA and even wrote her name on the rover's side.

In 2011, the Curiosity rover finally began its journey to Mars, with Clara's name on the side. Eight months later, after traveling the 53.7 million miles from Earth to Mars, Curiosity landed on the red planet and began its essential work.

You might wonder why we need to send a rover to a faraway planet. The answer is simple: We want to know if there is or was life on Mars. By studying the planet's climate and geology, Curiosity will help us answer that question.

Amazingly, 10 years after landing on Mars, Curiosity is still operational today.

Wolfgang Amadeus Mozart

AUSTRIAN MUSICIAN & COMPOSER

Wolfgang Amadeus Mozart was a masterful composer, musician, and performer. His music continues to inspire people centuries after his death.

Do you like music? Perhaps you listen to pop, rock, EDM, or hip-hop. Whichever style of music is your favorite, it is probably made using modern technology such as computers and digital recording devices.

But once upon a time, before music videos and any technology to record music were invented, music was very different. In the 18th century, classical music styles such as opera, choral music, symphonies, concertos, and chamber music ruled Europe. A young musical prodigy from Salzburg, Austria, Wolfgang Amadeus Mozart was one of the biggest stars of his day.

Today, he is considered one of the greatest composers of Western classical music. Thought by many to be a musical genius, he was able to play the harpsichord and keyboard from the age of three. He started composing at the age of five. By age six, he was touring Europe as a concert pianist, performing for royalty, ambassadors, and nobility. He was so young when he wrote his first pieces of music that his father had to help him — not with the music itself, but to hold the pen.

Wolfgang composed his first symphony at the age of nine and his first opera, "Mitridate, re di Ponto," when he was 14. When it premiered, the audience chanted "Long live the little maestro" in honor of the young composer.

Wolfgang's dad, Leopold, was also a composer and musician known for his own violin playing, musical compositions, and skills as a music teacher. Leopold taught his son Wolfgang to play instruments and compose music, along with his daughter Nannerl, who was also a musical prodigy.

But while Leopold was a talented musician in his own right, he could tell from a young age that his son would surpass him. He once described Wolfgang as "the miracle which God let be born in Salzburg."

While Wolfgang's musical talent made him famous, it didn't always bring him joy. He toured constantly from a very young age, practiced religiously, and worked incredibly hard to succeed.

While he was serious about music, Wolfgang wasn't very serious about much else. Those who have studied his life describe him as a rebellious, free-spirited person who spoke his mind, even when doing so got him into trouble. He was also known to have an offbeat sense of humor that offended some of the important people he played for.

In many ways, he was the rock star of his day. He was famous all over Europe, his concerts were always sold out, and he was mobbed by fans wherever he went.

Wolfgang composed around 600 works in his lifetime, including some of the most popular and well-known pieces of classical music. Even today, his music is still hugely popular all over the world. His work has been featured in movies, TV shows, and commercials, and his music continues to inspire new generations of musicians and composers.

Sadly, Wolfgang fell ill from an unknown illness and passed away at age 35. In his final year, despite his condition, he composed some of his most famous works, including the opera "The Magic Flute."

Even though he died relatively young, Wolfgang Amadeus Mozart left behind a legacy that inspired generations of musicians and will continue to do so for many years.

There is sometimes a misconception that geniuses are born, not made, meaning people like Wolfgang Amadeus Mozart are simply born with a natural talent and don't have to work hard to achieve success. But the truth is, even geniuses must put in years of practice and dedication to hone their craft.

That's what makes Mozart so inspiring.

His greatness resulted from a combination of his natural talent, creativity, and the countless hours he devoted to perfecting his skills.

Of course, the best way to learn about Wolfgang Amadeus Mozart is to listen to his music. If you've never heard his compositions, find a relaxing place, put on some earphones, and listen to some Mozart. You'll quickly see why his music inspires people centuries after his death.

And if you're ever feeling discouraged, remember that even geniuses work hard to achieve greatness.

Keep practicing, and never give up on your dreams.

Becky Schroeder

AMERICAN INVENTOR OF GLO-SHEET

Becky Schroeder invented Glo-sheet and became one of the youngest inventors to receive a US patent.

Many kids are scared of the dark, but 11-year-old Becky Schroeder is not one of them. In fact, she's using the power of darkness to help people all over the world.

Becky is the inventor of Glo-sheet, a special sheet that goes underneath a paper and emits a soft light. This makes it possible to write in the dark without using a flashlight, which can be disruptive to others.

Glo-sheet was inspired by Becky's experience of trying to finish her math homework in the car while her mom was shopping. It was dark outside and she couldn't see the paper well enough to write.

That's when Becky had her lightbulb moment. She realized that if she could find some way to light up the paper, she could finish her homework. Remembering her glow-in-the-dark toys from when she was younger, Becky had the idea to create a special sheet that would emit light.

With the help of her dad, Becky developed a prototype of a Glo-sheet using special paint that glows in the dark after being exposed to light for a short time. The idea was an immediate hit. It was perfect for people who worked in low-light conditions, like nurses and airplane pilots. Even NASA was interested in using Glo-sheet for future space missions!

WHEN BECKY WAS 12, SHE BECAME ONE OF THE YOUNGEST INVENTORS TO RECEIVE A US PATENT FOR HER INVENTION.

Glo-sheet is just one example of how a simple idea can make a big difference. As Becky Schroeder proves, with a little creativity, anyone can be an inventor — no matter how young they are!

WHAT WILL YOU INVENT?

Frank Epperson

Frank Epperson's accidental invention, the Popsicle, has become a beloved summertime treat around the globe.

Sometimes it's an accident that leads to a great invention. That's what happened to Frank Epperson.

Frank Epperson was born in 1894 in San Francisco, California. When he was just 11 years old, he had an accident that would change his life forever.

Frank was making a soda at home, using powdered mix and water. He mixed up the ingredients and added some sticks to use as stirrers. Then, he forgot about it and left the concoction on the porch overnight. The temperature dropped, and when Frank went to check on his drink the following day, he found that it had turned into a solid mass.

Frank had accidentally invented something called "frozen soda." He didn't think much of it at the time, but years later, he realized that he was onto something big.

In 1923, Frank applied for a patent for his invention. He started selling frozen sodas at fairs and carnivals, and they were a hit! He called his creation the "Eppsicle." He later changed the name to "Popsicle," and the rest is history.

Today, Popsicles are a summertime favorite all over the world — and it all started with one boy's accident.

Next time you enjoy a Popsicle on a hot day, remember Frank Epperson and his accidental invention.

Sometimes, it's the mistakes and accidents that lead to the greatest discoveries.

The key is to never give up. As author Tony Robbins said:

"No matter how many mistakes you make or how slow you progress, you are still way ahead of everyone who isn't trying."

Ryan Hreljac

CANADIAN WATER ACTIVIST

At age six, Ryan Hreljac dedicated himself to providing clean water for those in need. He has since gone on to help almost a million people worldwide with his "Ryan's Well Foundation."

Most of us don't think too much about water. We turn on the tap, and there it is. But not everyone is lucky enough to have safe, clean drinking water. For millions of people around the world, clean water isn't something you can get just from a faucet.

Ryan Hreljac, a six-year-old boy from Canada, was inspired to take action when he learned that kids in Africa had to walk miles each day to fetch water that was often contaminated.

Ryan's work as a water activist had humble beginnings. He did household chores to raise money for a company that provides clean water to underprivileged people called "WaterCan," collecting a total of $70 in his first four months.

But after a year, he'd grown his fund to $2,000 — enough to build a well in Africa. And a year later, he had raised $61,000. Realizing that Ryan was raising incredible amounts of money, the Canadian International Development Agency committed to donating $2 for every dollar Ryan raised.

By now, Ryan's work was earning him praise and attention. But this was just the beginning for the young activist. In 2001, at age 10, he started "Ryan's Well Foundation."

Initially, Ryan's foundation educated children about the importance of clean water and sanitation. It soon expanded to provide clean water by building wells.

By 2015, Ryan's charity had implemented 900 water and sanitation projects, improving the lives of more than 800,000 people in 16 countries. Some of these projects involved installing rain harvesting tanks to help people access clean water while also helping the environment by minimizing water wastage.

As an adult, Ryan continues his incredible work with his foundation. His approach is very hands-on. He travels in person to countries across the globe to train the people there on how to look after their wells so they can continue to deliver clean drinking water to families in need.

Ryan Hreljac is a true example of how even young kids can have a significant impact.

His selfless dedication to helping others has benefitted almost a million people worldwide. Ryan has proven that anyone, regardless of age, can be a change agent and create a better world.

Abbey Fleck

AMERICAN INVENTOR OF MAKIN' BACON

Abbey Fleck invented Makin' Bacon, a revolutionary way to cook bacon in the microwave without making a mess.

At just eight years old, Abbey was already showing signs of being a budding entrepreneur. She loved coming up with new ideas and inventions and always looked for ways to make things better or more efficient.

One day, while helping her dad cook bacon, she had a lightbulb moment. She thought, "There has to be a better way to cook bacon without making such a mess." That's when the idea for Makin' Bacon was born.

Abbey researched and found that no products on the market did what she wanted her invention to do, so she decided to make it herself!

With the help of her dad, Abbey designed and built a prototype of Makin' Bacon. The idea was simple. It was a tray with ridges that would cook the bacon in the microwave without splattering grease everywhere.

They took it to a local trade show, and it was a huge hit! People loved the idea, and Abbey started getting orders from all over the country.

At just nine years old, Abbey became a successful entrepreneur — and she hasn't looked back since. Makin' Bacon is now sold in stores across the United States and Abbey has appeared on popular TV shows like Oprah and David Letterman.

ABBEY'S EXPERIENCE PROVES THAT ANYONE CAN ACHIEVE THEIR DREAMS, NO MATTER HOW BIG OR SMALL.

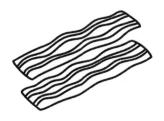

Activity - Finish the Pictures

Creativity can be a helpful tool to help you think outside the box and find solutions to any challenges that come your way. And, like anything, creativity is a skill that can be developed and improved with practice!

In this activity, you will explore your creative side by finishing the pictures on the next page. It's easy — just look at the incomplete drawings and use your imagination to complete them. You could add color or extra details or even create a story about what's happening in the picture.

Remember, there is no right or wrong answer — this activity should be fun and help you to tap into your creative thinking skills.

Once you have finished each picture, take a step back and look at it as a whole. What story does the picture tell? How did you use creativity to solve the problem presented by the unfinished images?

This activity is a great way to practice your creative thinking skills and get into the habit of looking for solutions when faced with a challenge. It will also help you to develop your imagination and have fun!

Remember, don't give up — use creativity to find solutions!

Finish the PICTURES

Turn the following into complete images

PERSEVERANCE AND DETERMINATION

PUSHING THROUGH CHALLENGES TO ACHIEVE IMPOSSIBLE DREAMS

PERSEVERANCE

is **failing**

19 TIMES and

SUCCEEDING

the 20th.

— Julie Andrews

Do you ever feel like giving up? Do you sometimes find it hard to stay focused on your goal or task, even when there are distractions or setbacks? If so, then you probably understand the importance of determination.

DETERMINATION IS THE INNER DRIVE AND FOCUS THAT KEEPS US MOTIVATED, EVEN IN DIFFICULT AND UNCERTAIN TIMES.

It's the ability to stay focused on our goals and keep pushing forward, despite life's challenges. It's a combination of resilience, hard work, and dedication — all of which are necessary for success in any field.

Determination is like riding a bicycle up a steep hill. You might struggle and feel like giving up, but if you keep pedaling, you'll eventually make it to the top. Just like riding a bike, determination will help you overcome any obstacle and reach success. You just need to keep pushing forward and never give up!

This chapter will explore the stories of incredible young people who have shown remarkable perseverance and determination. We'll learn how their refusal to give up has helped them achieve their goals, overcome challenges, and make a difference in the world. We will also consider how perseverance can help us face our struggles and keep going when times are tough.

By the end of this chapter, you'll have a greater understanding of why determination is an important quality to cultivate in order to succeed!

THIS CHAPTER WILL SERVE AS A REMINDER THAT NO MATTER HOW DIFFICULT THINGS MAY SEEM IF YOU KEEP GOING AND NEVER GIVE UP, YOU CAN ACHIEVE ANYTHING.

Get ready to be inspired by the fantastic stories of these courageous young people who have shown us how powerful perseverance can be!

Max Woosey

ENGLISH FUNDRAISER

Max Woosey's two-year camping effort raised over $780,000 for a local hospice, making a massive impact on their patients and families.

Do you like camping? Maybe you've been on a camping trip with your family or friends. You might have even camped in your backyard. But after a few nights of sleeping in a tent, you probably returned to your comfortable bed indoors.

Now imagine that you had to camp all the time outdoors, even when it was cold and raining. That's what Max Woosey did for two years to raise money for a local charity.

Max is from England, and when he was 10, his neighbor and friend, a 74-year-old man named Rick who was battling cancer, gave Max his tent and said, "Promise me you'll have an adventure in there."

A short while later, Rick passed away. Max was determined to honor Rick's life and make good on his promise. So, he began an adventure that would see him spend over 700 nights in a tent.

Max wanted to thank the North Devon Hospice, who had cared for his friend Rick before he died. The hospice relies on donations, so Max decided to raise money for them by camping out and asking people to sponsor him.

Around the same time, the COVID-19 pandemic hit, and Max realized that the hospice would be even more in need of donations because of the sudden lockdowns. So, he set up a JustGiving page and started camping to raise money while making good on the promise he had made to Rick.

Starting in March 2020, Max camped every single night outdoors for two years. He slept in his tent in all weather conditions, including Storm Eunice, a massive storm that broke records with winds of 122 miles per hour. He battled through two cold winters when temperatures dropped below freezing and sweated through heat waves in the summer when temperatures reached over 30 degrees Celsius. He slept in his tent on his birthday, Christmas Eve, and New Year's Eve, going through 12 tents during his adventure.

While most of his camping was in his garden at home, as interest in his adventure grew, he received invitations to camp in other locations. He camped in the garden at 10 Downing Street in London (where the British Prime Minister lives), at London Zoo, and on the pitch at the 80,000 national stadium. When Max received awards for his incredible fundraising efforts, he camped out on the balcony or roof of the hotel he was staying at with his family.

By the end of 2021, his fundraising page had raised a massive £680,000 (over $780,000) in donations. The hospice was blown away by his efforts and said the money would employ 20 nurses for a year and make a "huge difference" to the patients and families they cared for.

Max showed great determination and resilience in camping out every night for two years, no matter the weather. "There have been lots of nights of horrible weather — times when it's raining or freezing — and you want to go inside, but you think, 'No, I'm out here raising money, it's a good cause.' You've got to keep on fighting," he said.

In March 2022, at the age of 12, after spending a full two years camping outside every night, Max finally ended his adventure and came indoors. His family was quite relieved. They were very proud of Max's accomplishments but were looking forward to living as a typical family for a while.

Max says he'll still spend plenty of nights in his tent at home and is looking forward to a "proper adventure" one day, perhaps in Madagascar or Australia.

Max's story is incredible and a great example of the importance of never giving up.

NO MATTER HOW HARD STAYING OUTSIDE IN A TENT GOT, MAX KEPT GOING.

In doing so, he raised an astonishing amount of money for a cause that was very important to him.

His late friend Rick would be very proud and would undoubtedly agree that Max went on an incredible journey.

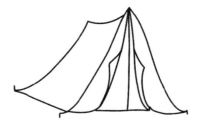

Melati and Isabel Wijsen

INDONESIAN CLIMATE CHANGE ACTIVISTS

Melati and Isabel Wijsen used their voices to successfully secure a ban on plastic bags in Bali. Now they are inspiring people worldwide to join their fight against single-use plastics.

Did you know that humans use around 1.2 million plastic bottles every minute? And only 9% of those bottles are recycled?

Since plastic was first introduced in the 1950s, we have produced 8.3 billion tons of plastic, and almost all of it still exists in some form.

Plastic pollution is now one of the biggest environmental crises facing our planet. It's estimated that at least 14 million tons of the plastic we use end up in the oceans yearly, where marine animals get tangled in it or eat it, causing diseases and injury. Even more of the plastic ends up in landfills, where it contaminates soil and water and can cause harm to animals.

The Wijsen sisters were so shocked by these statistics and what they learned at school that they decided to do something about it. Their goal is "to rid the world of single-use plastics," which is any plastic or plastic packaging we use only once before throwing away.

In 2013, when Melati Wijsen was only 12 years old and her sister Isabel was just 10, the pair started a campaign called "Bye Bye Plastic Bags." They began petitioning the government of their home country, Bali, to ban plastic bags. Their movement quickly gained momentum and managed to get over 50,000 signatures. As a result of their efforts, the government of Bali committed to phasing out plastic bags by 2018 and agreed to ban single-use plastics by 2022.

"Bye Bye Plastic Bags" became "Bye Bye Plastics." By now, it wasn't just a campaign — it was an organization making a difference in 29 countries around the globe. Through their work, Melati and Isabel are on a mission to have single-use plastics banned worldwide.

The sisters found new ways to reduce single-use plastics in Indonesia. They founded Mountain Mamas, a project that trains women in Bali to make reusable bags from recycled plastic. They also spread their message on major global platforms such as TED, CNN, and the United Nations.

Their efforts have not gone unnoticed. The sisters have been awarded numerous accolades. In 2017, Forbes Magazine named Melati as one of the 10 most inspiring women in Indonesia. Then, in 2018, Time magazine listed the sisters as two of the 25 Most Influential Teens in the World. In 2020, Melati was invited to speak at the World Economic Forum in Davos.

Today, Melati is 24 years old and Isabel is 22. On their journey to make the world a safer place for its animals and people, the pair transformed from ambitious tweens into innovative teen-agers and now two self-assured adults, playing a leading role in steering the world towards a better future.

Bye Bye Plastics now has a presence in 60 countries, and the sisters have also started YOUTHTOPIA. This platform educates young people about problems in the world, such as climate change and inequality. It aims to create young leaders willing to drive positive change in the world.

The story of Melati and Isabel is incredibly inspiring. It illustrates how a new generation of young people is stepping up to take ac-tion and create a sustainable, safer, and kinder world for future generations.

IF THESE TWO SISTERS CAN CHANGE THE WORLD,

SO CAN YOU.

As Melati told an audience at the WEF annual meeting in 2020,

"YOU'RE NEVER TOO YOUNG TO MAKE A DIFFERENCE, AND IT'S NOT TOO LATE TO TAKE ACTION."

Judit Polgar

Judit Polgar is a Hungarian chess prodigy who became the youngest grandmaster at 15.

In 2020, a Netflix series about a young female chess prodigy called "The Queen's Gambit" was a huge hit. While the show is fictional, there is a real-life chess champion who has been achieving amazing things since an early age, and her name is Judit Polgar.

Judit has astonished people with her chess skills since long before she was a tween. At age five, she defeated a family friend without looking at the board. At age seven, she visited the main square of Kecskemét, in her home country of Hungary, where people would gather to play chess. She took on 15 opponents at the same time and defeated each one.

By the time she was a tween, Judit was proving herself a chess prodigy by bettering male opponents with far more experience than her. At 11, she defeated an international chess master, Dolfi Drimer. When

she was 12, she got the better of Lev Gutman, a grandmaster, the highest title in chess.

BY AGE 15, JUDIT WAS A GRANDMASTER HERSELF, BECOMING THE YOUNGEST PERSON TO EVER ACHIEVE THIS TITLE.

While chess is male-dominated, Judit fought for her belief that it didn't have to be. She believed that chess champions should not be divided by gender, as it's an intellectual game and women and men are intellectual equals.

In fact, Judit is using chess to help people build the skills they need to excel in STEM subjects — science, technology, engineering, and mathematics. Since retiring from professional chess in 2015, she has devoted her life to inspiring more girls, and people in general, to play the game she is passionate about.

Judit is an inspiration.

BY COMPETING AS AN EQUAL IN A MALE-DOMINATED GAME, SHE PROVED THAT YOU CAN ACHIEVE ANYTHING YOU SET YOUR MIND TO WITH ENOUGH FOCUS AND DETERMINATION.

Jordan Romero

With his incredible feat of becoming the youngest person in history to climb Mount Everest and later the seven summits, Jordan Romero has inspired a new generation of young adventurers and changemakers.

Can you imagine standing on top of the world and enjoying the view from the highest mountain on Earth after braving hurricane-force winds to get there?

For most of us, it's just a dream (or a nightmare). But for Jordan Romero, it was reality. On May 22, 2010, at the age of 13, Jordan fulfilled his lifelong dream and became the youngest person to reach the summit of Mount Everest.

A year and a half later, in December 2011, at 15, he became the youngest to complete the seven summits. The seven summits are the highest peaks on the world's seven continents. Climbing all seven summits is regarded as one of the toughest challenges in mountain climbing.

By the time Jordan summited Everest in 2010, he had already completed five of the seven summits.

He started with Mount Kilimanjaro in Africa when he was 10 years old before scaling Australia's highest mountain, Kosciuszko, a year later.

Three months after this, Jordan reached the top of Europe's highest mountain, Russia's Mount Elbrus. In the same year, he also found time to scale Argentina's Aconcagua, the highest peak in South America. Then, in 2008, at the age of 12, he made it to his fifth major peak, Denali, in Alaska, at the northernmost point of his home country, the United States.

 To complete the seven peaks, he traveled to Antarctica, the coldest and remotest of the earth's continents, to climb Mount Vinson.

This is a lot of adventure for someone so young, but Jordan wasn't alone. Two of his climbing mates are his father, Paul, a helicopter medic, and his stepmother Karen, an athlete and member of the US National Alpine Skiing Team.

Karen and Paul are no strangers to adventure, as they compete in an adventure racing sport that combines paddling, climbing, and biking. Competitions last a week and take place in remote parts of the wilderness.

While Jordan loved the experience of climbing Mount Everest with his dad and stepmom, he must have missed his mom,

Leigh-Anne. When he got to the peak of Everest, the first thing Jordan did was call her. In an interview for ABC News, she said she trusted her son and didn't believe he would ever take unnecessary risks while trying to achieve his goals.

However, not everyone was supportive of Jordan's adventures. Some high-profile mountain climbers and medical advisers believed he was too young to climb Everest. Not everyone who mounts the world's highest mountain makes it back alive. In fact, each year, on average, five climbers die attempting to summit Everest. Some people felt Jordan should have been made to wait until he was older.

Some were critical of the way Jordan and his team climbed Everest, too. The mountain can be reached from two countries, Nepal and Tibet. The mountain's north face in Tibet is much harder to climb than the south side in Nepal. But Nepal doesn't allow people younger than 16 to attempt to scale Everest, so Jordan and his team were forced to do the more challenging climb from the Tibetan side.

After Jordan's incredible feat, the Chinese government imposed an age limit of 16 on the Tibetan side of Everest. This means no one will ever officially have the opportunity to break Jordan's record.

While some may have been critical of the lengths Jordan went to in achieving his dreams, he has the support of his mom, dad, and stepmom, which has allowed him to climb to heights that few people his age would get a chance to.

JORDAN'S DREAM WAS TO 'STAND ON TOP OF THE WORLD,' AND THROUGH INCREDIBLE FOCUS AND DEDICATION, HE WAS ABLE TO ACHIEVE IT.

What's your dream? Perhaps if you work hard enough to make it a reality, it can come true, just like Jordan's did.

Inge Sørensen

DANISH SWIMMING CHAMPION

Inge Sørensen became the youngest person to win an Olympic medal and inspired young people everywhere to pursue their dreams.

Imagine competing in the biggest event of your life in front of thousands of people. Now imagine doing it when you're just 12 years old.

This is precisely what Inge Sørensen did in 1936 when she competed in the Olympic Games in Berlin. And what's more, she came third, winning a bronze medal in her event, the 200-meter breaststroke!

Inge's story is one of determination and hard work. She started swimming when she was three years old. By the time she was 11, she was already a national champion. In those days, access to pools was limited, so Inge often had to swim in the cold, outdoor water of the harbor in the sea near her house.

Despite the challenges, she continued to train hard and soon caught the attention of the Danish Olympic team. After becoming the national champion at just 11, she was selected for the 1936 Olympic Games.

She knew it would be a tough competition when she qualified for the Olympics. Inge was not deterred, though. After winning her heat, she gave it her all in the 200-meter breaststroke final and came third. She was the youngest person ever to win an Olympic medal! And to this day, nobody younger has won an Olympic medal in any sport or discipline.

Inge's achievements are all the more impressive when you consider that she was competing against women who were twice her age.

She continued to compete and broke several world records. Her career ended when the Second World War began and the two following Olympics were canceled.

INGE'S STORY IS ONE OF INSPIRATION AND HOPE. IT SHOWS US THAT NO MATTER HOW YOUNG YOU ARE, YOU CAN ACHIEVE GREAT THINGS IF YOU SET YOUR MIND TO IT.

Emma Watson

Emma Watson is the English actor who played the role of Hermione Granger in the Harry Potter films.

What would it feel like to be chosen to bring one of the most beloved characters in one of the most successful series of books of all time to life on the big screen?

Many people dream of becoming a Hollywood star. Emma Watson's dream became a reality at 11 when she was cast as Hermione Granger, the gifted young witch from JK Rowling's "Harry Potter" books.

Emma had dreamed of being an actor since she was six. But while she had appeared in a few school plays, she had never acted professionally before she co-starred in "Harry Potter and the Sorcerer's Stone" in 2001.

Rather than calling on young professional actors to audition, the casting team searched for children perfect for the film's starring roles.

While anyone who has seen the films probably couldn't imagine anyone else as Hermione, the role was not handed to her straight away. She auditioned eight times before being chosen over thousands of other girls. Emma says that while her parents tried to prepare her for disappointment in case she didn't get the part, she was determined to do anything it took to get it.

"Harry Potter and the Sorcerer's Stone" became an instant hit when it was released in 2001. The film not only made it into the list of the top 50-grossing movies of all time but was also loved by critics and audiences alike. Emma was widely praised for her role and became an icon, inspiring girls around the globe.

While some film franchises struggle to maintain the momentum of their first film, the Harry Potter movies were all massive commercial and critical successes. The final film of the series, "Harry Potter and the Deathly Hallows Part 2," became the series' biggest hit.

In the end, eight Harry Potter movies were made. Filming was a decade-long journey for Emma and her co-stars Daniel Radcliffe, who played Harry, and Rupert Grint, who played Ron Weasly. The trio grew up on the sets of the films, transforming from inexperienced children in their debut to self-assured adults in the final film.

While many young actors struggle to keep up with their schooling, Emma took her education seriously. She was determined not to fall behind due to her acting success. She achieved consistently high grades with help from tutors on the set of the films. After the final two films were shot, she studied at Brown College, where she earned a degree in English literature.

Emma's time as Hermione was only the first chapter of her remarkable story. In 2014, at 24 years of age, she was appointed a United Nations goodwill ambassador. She began traveling the globe to promote equal rights for women. She helped launch "HeForShe," an initiative involving men and boys in the fight for gender equality.

Emma has also promoted animal welfare and fair trade, a system that helps make conditions better for workers around the world, as well as for the environment. In 2016, she became an ambassador for Camfed, which works to educate girls in rural parts of Africa and end the practice of children being forced into marriage.

Even when she was still shooting the Harry Potter movies, Emma had begun her journey as an activist. At the age of 19, she learned about problems in the fashion industry, such as child labor, the exploitation of animals, and the considerable carbon impact fashion companies have on the world.

In response, she launched a fashion range in collaboration with "People Tree," a sustainable clothing company. Soon afterward, she launched her own organic clothing line in part-nership with famous fashion designer Alberta Ferretti.

Emma's humanitarian, activist, and fashion designer work hasn't slowed her acting career. She has appeared in 19 films, including critically acclaimed roles in "The Perks of Being a Wallflower," "Beauty and the Beast," and "Little Women."

Emma Watson is more than just an accomplished actor; she inspires millions. While she could have rested on her laurels as a Hollywood star, she chose instead to use her fame to inspire positive change.

EMMA COMBINES AN INCREDIBLE WORK ETHIC WITH A DESIRE TO IMPROVE THE WORLD AND A PASSIONATE COMMITMENT TO DOING THINGS HER WAY.

And all of this started when she was a tween.

She once said, "I don't want other people to decide who I am. I can do that for myself".

Activity - Things You Won't Ever Give Up On

Sometimes we all need a bit of extra motivation to keep going and never give up on our dreams.

But to channel our determination, we sometimes need to take a step back and remind ourselves of all that's important to us.

This exercise will help you identify the things you are most passionate about and will never give up on.

To complete this activity:
- Think about the things that are really important to you. This could be anything from getting good grades to making a difference in the world. It could include activities, causes, values, or anything else important to you.
- Write them down on paper (or on the next page).
- For each item you have written down, write at least one sentence about why it's important and why you won't ever give up on it.

Once you've completed the exercise, hang the list somewhere you can see it often — it could be on the wall in your bedroom or the fridge!

This activity can also be a reminder when times get tough and you feel like giving up. It can help you stay focused, determined, and motivated to never give up on your dreams!

We hope this activity helps you to believe in yourself and take action toward making a difference.

THINGS (YOU)

won't ever give up...

🙂 I will never give up ....

OPTIMISM

SEEING POSSIBILITIES WHERE
OTHERS SEE LIMITATIONS

Every NEW DAY begins with POSSIBILITIES.

- Ronald Reagan

We all face difficult times in life, but how we choose to respond can make a huge difference. Having an optimistic outlook can be the key to success when faced with adversity.

Optimism means approaching each challenge positively and seeing it as an opportunity rather than an obstacle.

It's believing things will eventually work out, even if the situation seems bleak. It's having faith that you will find a way through any difficulty and that good things can come from bad experiences.

In this chapter, we will explore stories of young people who have faced tough times but managed to stay positive to achieve their goals. We will also consider how having an optimistic outlook can help us to view challenging situations as chances for growth and development.

By the end of this chapter, you'll have a greater understanding of why optimism is an important quality to cultivate in order to succeed!

Sky Brown

Sky Brown became the youngest ever Team GB athlete to compete at an Olympic Games, inspiring young people worldwide to pursue their passions.

For many young people, skateboarding is a fun way to get around town and spend time with friends. But imagine if you could turn your love of skating into a career. That's precisely what Sky Brown has done. At 14 years old, the British-Japanese girl is the world's youngest professional skater and surfer, and she's just getting started!

Tony Hawk, who many consider to be one of the best pro skateboarders of all time, described Sky as a "unicorn" and "one of the best female skaters ever."

In 2021, Sky became Great Britain's youngest-ever Olympic medalist when she won bronze in skateboarding at the Tokyo Olympics. Amazingly, she almost didn't make it.

Firstly, she had to convince her parents to let her compete, as they were concerned about the pressure on their daughter.

Secondly, Sky almost didn't make it to the Games. Skating can be dangerous. Sky knows this all too well after she fell from a halfpipe ramp while training for the Olympics in May 2020, suffering several skull fractures and a broken hand and wrist. Her father said she was "lucky to be alive" after she was airlifted to hospital and was unresponsive when she arrived.

This wasn't Sky's first skateboarding accident. She broke her arm while competing in her first Olympic qualifying event in 2019. While many people would have given up after this, Sky simply got back on her skateboard, winning first place while competing with her arm in a cast.

But these accidents didn't keep Sky down for long or discourage her from attempting to become an Olympic medalist. In June 2021, she was selected to represent Britain at the 2020 Olympics, which was postponed to July 2021 due to the COVID-19 pandemic.

Not content to stick to one sport, Sky is also an avid surfer. She has set her sights on representing Team GB in skating and surfing at the 2024 Olympics in Paris.

Sky has entertained crowds on her skateboard since she was eight when she competed in the US Open. Skating isn't just a sport to Sky — it's her passion. She hopes that by achieving her dreams and goals, she can inspire others to do the same.

"When I skate, I just feel free, like I can do anything," she once said. "And if people see me, the smallest girl, doing the highest trick, then anyone could think they could do anything."

Sky's single-minded focus on her skating and surfing and her determination to succeed serve as an inspiration to other young people with big dreams.

ACCORDING TO SKY, ALL YOU NEED TO DO TO ACHIEVE YOUR DREAMS IS BELIEVE IN YOURSELF.

After becoming an Olympic medalist, Sky had this to say:

"I really hope I inspire some girls. I feel like people think I'm too young and I can't do it, but, if you believe in yourself, you can do anything. I believed in myself and I'm here."

Samantha Smith

Samantha Smith changed the world by becoming the youngest American ambassador to Russia and improving relations between the United States and the Soviet Union with her message of peace.

In the early 1980s, the United States and Russia were locked in a Cold War. Relations between the two countries were tense, and many feared a nuclear war.

Into this charged atmosphere came Samantha Smith, a young girl from Maine, USA, with a message of peace.

Samantha became interested in Russian culture after she saw a news report about Russian soldiers in Afghanistan. She was only 10 years old at the time, but she was already worried about the possibility of nuclear war.

Samantha decided to write a letter to Soviet leader Yuri Andropov, expressing her concerns. She asked him, "Are you going to vote to have a war?" and went on to say, "God made the world for us to share and take care of. Not to fight over..."

To Samantha's surprise, Andropov wrote back! He thanked her for her letter and explained that the Soviet Union had no intention of starting a war. He also invited her to visit the Soviet Union.

In July of 1983, Samantha and her family traveled to Moscow. Her trip to the Soviet Union was a media sensation. She spent two weeks there, touring the country and staying at a school where she learned Russian songs and lived with other kids her age.

Although Samantha's trip was brief, it had a lasting impact. She became known as the "youngest American ambassador to Russia." Although she didn't end the Cold War with her visit, in a small way, she did help to improve relations between the United States and the Soviet Union.

Sadly, Samantha passed away in 1985 at 13, but her legacy of peace lives on.

SAMANTHA SMITH SHOWED THE WORLD THAT EVEN A YOUNG PERSON CAN MAKE A DIFFERENCE. ALL IT TAKES IS ONE SMALL ACT OF KINDNESS TO MAKE THE WORLD A BETTER PLACE.

Savanna Lorpu Karmue

AMERICAN HEALTHY HEART ACTIVIST

Savanna Lorpu Karmue is an inspiring young activist dedicated to promoting heart health and fighting childhood obesity.

The heart is one of the most essential organs in the human body. Every second or so, it pumps blood to every part of the body. That's a lot of work! But the heart is a bit like an engine — it needs the right fuel to keep running. And we all know what happens when you put the wrong fuel in an engine — it won't work correctly! The same is true for hearts. They will only work efficiently if you feed them healthy food and drinks.

Savanna Lorpu Karmue understands the importance of healthy eating and exercise to maintain a healthy heart. She has become an advocate for healthy living, promoting more nutritious food choices for young people and raising awareness about the dangers of childhood obesity.

It all started when Savanna's Sunday school teacher underwent heart surgery at the local hospital. Savanna was only eight years old, but the experience significantly impacted her. Her teacher told her that she had to visit a cardiologist — a doctor specializing in the human heart. Savanna was fascinated and decided she wanted to be a cardiologist someday.

Savanna started researching the heart and learned that 2,000 people die daily from heart disease. So, when she was eight years old, she started making YouTube videos promoting healthy eating and exercise to maintain a healthy heart.

Soon, she had her own non-profit organization, "Happy Heart Advice." In 2016, when Savanna was 10, she launched the first of a series of "Happy Heart Challenges" and "The Happy Heart Program." These aimed to raise awareness of the importance of a healthy diet and lifestyle for children and families.

Savanna is now working on an app that will make it easier for parents to shop for "Happy Heart-Approved" food children can enjoy without compromising their health.

Today, Savanna is a speaker, entrepreneur, author, and health advocate helping to empower children to make healthier choices and spread the message of heart health.

SAVANNA IS AN INSPIRING EXAMPLE OF HOW YOUNG PEOPLE CAN MAKE A DIFFERENCE.

Her goal is a big one: She wants to halve the rate of obesity among children in America by 2031. Thanks to the fantastic hard work she has done already and the incredible dedication she has shown in her fight against child obesity, she may well achieve it.

Marley Dias

AMERICAN ACTIVIST & AUTHOR

Marley Dias successfully launched a viral social media campaign called "1000 Black Girl Books," collecting over 12,000 books with black female leads.

Reading is powerful. It's one of the ways many young people expand their horizons, enrich their lives, and learn about the world. In fact, since you're here, right now, reading this book, you probably know this already!

However, sometimes books aren't just about learning new things—they're also about reading stories you can relate to. When Marley was 11 years old, she found that most of the books she read featured white protagonists. As a young black American girl descended from Jamaica and Cape Verde, she wanted to see herself and her experiences reflected in literature. She soon discovered that many other young people, teachers, and parents felt the same way.

SO, SHE STARTED A CAMPAIGN CALLED #1000BlackGirlBooks. SHE AIMED TO COLLECT 1,000 BOOKS WITH BLACK FEMALE LEADS AND DONATE THEM TO SCHOOLS.

She launched a social media campaign and set up a crowd-funding page to help raise money for the cause. The movement gained traction quickly, and before she knew it, Marley's story had gone viral. Books were pouring in from around the world!

After just a few months, she collected over 9,000 books with young, black female lead characters. And soon afterward, she started donating them to schools in the US and Jamaica.

She has collected more than 13,000 books (and counting!) and has a database on her website for people who want to discover these books for themselves.

But Marley didn't stop there. She didn't want to just collect books from other people. She also wanted to inspire young people to make the world a better place and make their dreams come true. So, in 2019, she wrote a book of her own. "Marley Dias Gets It Done and So Can You," tells her story and maps out her vision for how young people can get involved in their communities and use social media for good.

As if all this isn't impressive enough, Marley has been involved in several other projects. She was made editor of her own online magazine in partnership with Elle. She created her own Netflix show, "Bookmarks: Celebrating Black Authors," in which she reads and discusses books with famous people. Not only is she the host of the show, but she is also its executive producer.

In 2021, she was made the ambassador for the US National Education Association's Read Across America program. She has spoken at the White House alongside Oprah Winfrey and Michelle Obama — and all of this before she turned 17!

Marley aims to promote books about black girls and help create a world where all people, whether white, black, Asian or Latinx, have a voice. It's not about silencing one person so that another can be heard but about allowing all kinds of people to express themselves and feel represented.

In 2022, Marley graduated from her high school in New Jersey and started studying at Harvard University. It's a safe bet that she will continue to find new ways to inspire people worldwide with her activism.

THROUGH THE INCREDIBLE WORK SHE STARTED WHEN SHE WAS JUST A TWEEN, MARLEY HAS SHOWN YOU'RE NEVER TOO YOUNG TO FIGHT FOR WHAT YOU BELIEVE IN AND CHANGE THE WORLD.

Michelle Wie

AMERICAN GOLF CHAMPION

Michelle Wie is a professional golfer who became a tournament champion at 11 years old and went on to play in and win numerous tournaments competing against both men and women.

Picture a golfer. What do you see? Many people would imagine a middle-aged man hitting balls off a manicured green. But Michelle Wie is different. She's a young woman who has been shattering stereotypes and making history in golf since she was a child.

Michelle was born in Honolulu, Hawaii, in 1989. When she was four years old, she started playing golf and quickly showed a natural talent for the sport. By the time she was eight, she was appearing on television shows and giving interviews about her love of golf.

But Michelle's rise to golfing fame really began when she was 10 years old. In 2000, she became the youngest player to qualify for a United States Golf Association (USGA) amateur competition. And this was just the start for the young trailblazer.

When she was 11, Michelle won two tournaments. A year later, when she was 12, she became the youngest to ever qualify for a Ladies Professional Golf Association (LPGA) event. In the same year, she became the youngest to play in an LPGA major, one of the most prestigious events in women's golfing.

But Michelle was not content to only compete against other young women. She wanted to test herself against the best golfers in the world, which meant playing against men and women.

In 2004, Michelle made history again by becoming the youngest female to compete in a Professional Golf Association of America (PGA) tour event. She scored 68, the best score ever by a woman in a PGA event. Although she didn't win that tournament, she proved that she could compete with the best golfers in the world, male or female.

Since then, Michelle has had a fantastic career as a professional golfer. She has won many tournaments, including the 2014 U.S. Women's Open. She was the first female player to make over $1 million in prize money in a single season.

In 2022, Michelle announced that she would be stepping away from her career in professional golf for a while. However, she didn't rule out returning to the game in the future.

While some believe she may have had more success if she had just played against women, Michelle has no regrets.

"I don't have any regrets because I feel like I've always learned from every mistake that I've made," she said. "I feel like even if it was a huge major fail, at least it makes for a good story now."

Michelle is a true pioneer in the world of golf. She has shown that women can compete with men in a traditionally male-dominated sport. She is an inspiration to young people, not only because of her record-setting achievements as a young golfer, but also because, throughout her career, she did things her way.

SHE PROVES THAT REMAINING TRUE TO YOURSELF AND DOING THINGS ON YOUR OWN TERMS ARE THE TWO GREATEST FORMS OF SUCCESS.

Activity - The Power of Positive Thinking

As we have seen from the stories in this chapter, one of the most important keys to success is having a positive outlook. A positive attitude can help you stay motivated and focused on your goals and make it easier to overcome any challenges that come your way.

In this activity, you will create a "positive thinking jar" — a fun and creative way to keep track of your positive thoughts.

To make your positive thinking jar:

- Get a jar or container — you could choose something like a mason jar, coffee tin, or an old shoe box!
- Decorate the inside and outside of your chosen vessel with inspiring quotes, symbols, colors, etc. Make it bright and colorful — and have fun with it!
- Once your jar is ready, you can start adding positive thoughts. You could write a list of things you are grateful for or add quotes, affirmations, and/or pictures. The options are endless!

This activity is a great way to remind yourself that you have the power to stay positive and motivated, no matter what life throws at you. Make sure to check in with your positive thinking jar from time to time — it can help you stay on track and keep striving towards achieving great things!

Remember — Always think positively and never give up!

The POSITVE thinking Jar

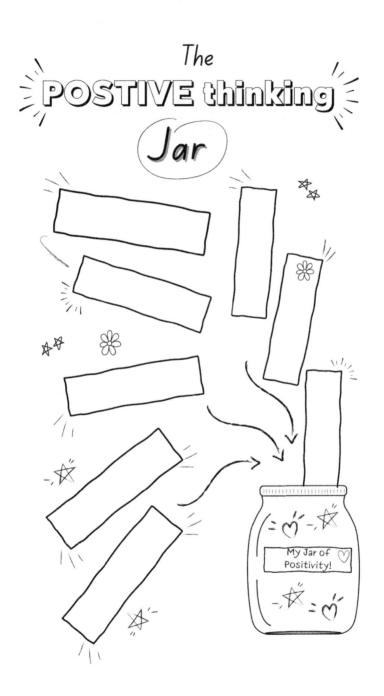

COMPASSION

FIGHTING FOR INJUSTICE AND HELPING THOSE IN NEED

COMPASSION
is THE GREATEST
form of LOVE
HUMANS HAVE
to offer.

- Rachael Joy Scott

Compassion means treating others with care and understanding, regardless of their background or circumstances. It's empathizing with those who have gone through different experiences than you and showing kindness even when it's difficult.

COMPASSION IS ESSENTIAL FOR CREATING POSITIVE RELATIONSHIPS AND BUILDING MEANINGFUL CONNECTIONS.

It helps us to understand different points of view, to work together with those who may disagree with us, and to show respect for all individuals.

This chapter will explore stories of young people who have shown compassion and how it helped them succeed. We'll also consider how having a compassionate outlook can bring about positive change in the world.

By the end of this chapter, you'll have a greater understanding of why compassion is an important quality to cultivate in order to succeed!

Nkosi Johnson

SOUTH AFRICAN HIV/AIDS ACTIVIST

Nkosi Johnson bravely advocated for greater compassion and understanding towards those living with HIV/AIDS, inspiring millions worldwide to stand up against stigma and discrimination.

Nkosi Johnson was born in 1989 in Johannesburg, South Africa. He was born with HIV, which attacks the immune system and can lead to AIDS. In those days, very little was known about HIV/AIDS, and there was a lot of stigma and misinformation surrounding the disease.

Nkosi was adopted by Gail Johnson after his birth mom, who also had the disease, became too ill to care for him.

Gail enrolled him in a local primary school when he was eight. This was a brave move, as many people believed that HIV/AIDS could be spread through casual contact. Initially, the school refused to accept him, but after a lengthy battle, Nkosi was finally allowed to attend.

Nkosi quickly became a well-known and much-loved figure in his community. In 1997, he was chosen to give a speech at the 13th International AIDS Conference.

In his speech, Nkosi called for greater understanding and acceptance of people living with HIV/AIDS. He also urged world leaders to do more to combat the disease.

Nkosi's message was simple but powerful: "We are normal. We have dreams and aspirations, like everyone else. All we ask is that you accept us and give us a chance."

Nkosi's speech was hailed as one of the most critical moments in the history of the AIDS pandemic. Tragically, Nkosi died just a few months later, at 12 years old.

However, his legacy lives on.

NKOSI'S MESSAGE OF UNDERSTANDING AND ACCEPTANCE CONTINUES TO INSPIRE PEOPLE ALL OVER THE WORLD.

In 2005, the United Nations named him a Messenger of Peace.

NO MATTER WHAT CHALLENGES WE FACE, WE SHOULD ALL STRIVE TO BE MORE LIKE NKOSI JOHNSON: BRAVE, COMPASSIONATE, AND KIND.

Nicholas Lowinger

AMERICAN HOMELESS "SHOE" ACTIVIST

Through Gotta Have Sole!, Nicholas Lowinger has provided over 30,000 pairs of shoes to those in need, inspiring and empowering countless young people to take action and make a difference.

Many of us don't spend a lot of time thinking about footwear. We take for granted that we have a pair of shoes to wear every day. But for some people, having shoes is a luxury they can't afford.

Enter Nicholas Lowinger. Nicholas noticed the importance shoes play for young people trying to fit in. Without them, many opportunities, like playing a sport or attending school, remain out of reach.

Nicholas was determined to change this. He wanted young people growing up homeless to have the same chances in life as other kids. As a result, when he was 12, he started the Gotta Have Sole Foundation, which donates new footwear to homeless children across America.

According to Nicholas, his interest in the plight of homeless children began when his mother took him to a homeless shelter when he was five. He noticed that many of the young people he met were barefoot or had shoes that were falling apart.

He heard heart-wrenching stories about young people who couldn't afford shoes. One boy was forced to share shoes with his sister and only attended school every second day. The shoes were sparkly and pink, which led to the boy being targeted by bullies. Other children he met had sores on their feet from wearing shoes that were the wrong size.

At the time, Nicholas donated his shoes and clothes to homeless shelters. But he wanted to make more of an impact, so he started Gotta Have Sole (GHS) in 2010.

By 2015, the organization had donated brand-new shoes to more than 42,000 kids in 36 US states. By 2019, over 100,000 kids in 50 US states had been gifted shoes by GHS. For many, it was the first pair of new shoes they had ever owned.

Nicholas partnered with big brands like Reebok, Puma, Timberland, and Hasbro, which all donated footwear to GHS. He also started a crowdfunding page to collect money for shoes through donations.

The boy he had previously met, who was forced to wear his sister's shoes was given a pair of brand-new basketball sneakers. This allowed him to regain his self-esteem, attend school every day, and work to achieve his dream of attending college. This is just one life that Nicholas touched through his charity.

GHS continues to grow, with 30 clubs spread across the United States. Aside from continuing to provide young, homeless people with shoes, the organization now has a scholarship program that gives those who don't have the finances an opportunity to go to college. GHS also launched an initiative called SOLEdiers, which provides new shoes to veterans living below the poverty line and their children.

For homeless children, having a pair of shoes they can feel proud of can be a game-changer. It may seem simple, but it gives them the confidence to participate in the same activities as their peers.

The story of Nicholas and GHS is a fantastic example of how small things can make a big difference. Simple, everyday items that many of us take for granted, like shoes, can mean the world to someone else.

FOR SOME YOUNG PEOPLE, THE JOURNEY TOWARD SUCCESS CAN START WITH SOMETHING AS SIMPLE AS A GOOD PAIR OF SHOES.

To learn more about the fantastic work that Nicholas is doing, go to *www.gottahavesole.org.*

Joshua Williams

AMERICAN FOOD ACTIVIST

Joshua Williams has raised millions of dollars to help provide meals to underprivileged people around the world through his organization, Joshua's Heart Foundation.

Hopefully you don't know what it's like to go to bed hungry. But sadly, millions of children around the globe experience this on a daily basis. They simply don't have access to food or clean drinking water.

When Joshua Williams was very young, he saw an advert about the world's starving children and it shocked him into action. Starting with a $20 donation from his grandma, Joshua set about raising money to end world hunger. Not long after, when he was just four years old, he founded Joshua's Heart Foundation. His foundation aimed to provide meals for underprivileged children and adults.

With his family's support, Joshua provided thousands of pounds of food to disadvantaged people in his home city of Miami, Florida.

Fast forward a few years and both Joshua and his foundation have grown. He is now 20, and his organization has 60,000 kids and 4,000 adults working as volunteers. Joshua's Heart has served over 4.9 million meals, raised over three million dollars, and helped an estimated 600,000 people.

Today, Joshua's organization doesn't just deliver food. It also teaches those who receive the food to prepare healthy meals. His work has earned him prestigious awards. He has been acknowledged by US presidents and has partnered with big companies like Disney and Unilever.

Maybe you want to help end world hunger. Why not become a volunteer for Joshua's Heart, join a similar organization in your own country, or start an organization just like Joshua did when he was only four?

Zach Bonner

AMERICAN PHILANTHROPIST

Zach Bonner is a true hero, inspiring people with his selfless-ness and determination to help homeless and impoverished children worldwide.

Imagine losing everything in a hurricane. Your home is destroyed, and you have to start completely over. When Zach Bonner saw the devastation caused by Hurricane Charley in his home state of Florida in 2004, he didn't just imagine the pain of those affected — he felt he had to do something about it.

So, Zach, only six years old at the time, started delivering water to families who had lost everything. He did this by walking around his neighborhood with a little red wagon. In the end, he delivered 27 pickup trucks of water. This was the beginning of Zach's commitment to helping others.

A year later, Zach founded his charity, "The Little Red Wagon Foundation," to help the 1.3 million children who are homeless or living in poverty in the US. His first project involved delivering 400 backpacks — or Zachpacks, as he called them — full of food, toiletries, and toys to homeless children. When Zach was eight, he received the Presidential Service Award from George W. Bush for his services to volunteering and helping others.

But Zach was only getting started. In 2007, he decided to begin walking to the White House to raise awareness about the plight of homeless children. In his first year, he covered 280 miles, from his home in Tampa to Tallahassee, on the other side of Florida.

Zach walked to Atlanta, Georgia, the following year, covering 250 miles. And in 2009, he walked a whopping 668 miles, making it to his final destination of Washington, DC.

But Zach wasn't done yet. Now 12 years old, he walked from Tampa to Los Angeles, California, covering 2,748 miles in just 178 days, an average of 20 miles a day! When he finally reached his destination, a hero's welcome awaited him. He was the youngest person ever to walk from the East Coast to the West Coast of the United States.

By now, Zach was famous. A film that tells his story, called "Little Red Wagon," was released. He received awards, appeared on "Good Morning America," and was invited to the White House by then-President George W Bush.

Fast forward to today and Zach is an adult who works in the tech industry. He loves to bake and you can often find him posting pics of his creations on social media.

But his commitment to helping homeless children continues. His Little Red Wagon Foundation continues to support children in need and fund other initiatives to help those in poverty.

Zach's inspiring story shows us that no one is too young to make a difference.

By channeling his concern for the homeless into action, he showed us all that one person can make a big difference, one step at a time.

Jahkil Jackson

AMERICAN ACTIVIST, AUTHOR & SPEAKER

Jahkil Jackson has founded and grown Project I Am to become a global organization providing necessities like food, water, toiletries, and clothing to those experiencing homelessness.

Not all people have a roof over their heads or a warm bed to sleep in at night. At eight years old, Jahkil Jackson felt he needed to do something to help the millions of homeless people in America. He started an organization called Project I Am to bring attention to the plight of the homeless.

Jahkil didn't just want to educate people about homelessness—he also wanted to take direct action. He started handing out "Blessings Bags" filled with first aid supplies, toiletries, medicine, and snacks. Not long after he gave out his 5,000th bag in 2017, former US President Barack Obama acknowledged Jahkil as one of the three people who "remind us what's best about America."

Today, at 14 years old, Jahkil continues to help the homeless and has become an influential author and speaker, inspiring young kids worldwide to become activists and entrepreneurs.

Despite his fantastic success, Jahkil has faced bullying. His first book, "I Am," talks about this and focuses on believing in yourself and ignoring negative influences. The book became a bestseller. Shortly after that, a second book, "Don't Wait to Be Great," also hit bestseller status. This time around, Jahkil's writing explored how young people can start their own businesses and projects to help people.

Jahkil doesn't only help and inspire people but is also a budding basketball player, tap dancer, and break dancer. With so many talents, it's no wonder that one of the greatest ever basketball players, LeBron James, asked Jahkil to join his Always Believe campaign.

He also caught the attention of Nike, and the company featured him in three separate campaigns. He was featured on Cartoon Network's "Drawn to Helping Others" show and CNN's "Heroes: Young Wonders" segment and was included in BET's list of "15 People Under 15."

Today, Jahkil is a public speaker. He continues to inspire thousands of people through his talks on finding your passion, setting goals, helping others, and being a positive influence.

JAHKIL SHOWS US THAT WHATEVER YOU WANT TO DO, WHETHER HELPING OTHERS OR FULFILLING YOUR DREAMS, THERE'S NO TIME TO WASTE.

Activity - Random Acts of Kindness Bingo

Being kind is one of the most important traits — it's an essential part of showing compassion and understanding toward others.

You will practice your kindness skills in this activity by playing Random Acts of Kindness Bingo. It's easy and fun – just look at the bingo board on the next page. Some of the squares are filled in, while others are blank. For the empty squares, write something you would like to do. It could be helping a neighbor with their grocery shopping, sending an encouraging text to a friend or family member, or even leaving a generous tip for your waiter!

Once you have chosen your kind acts, it's time to start playing. All you have to do is go out and do a random act of kindness each day. Once you have done the deed, tick off the corresponding square on your bingo board.

This activity helps you practice being kind and understanding to others and encourages you to see the good in others. Even a simple, thoughtful act can make someone's day!

Remember, kindness is an essential part of life, so spread some cheer by doing random acts of kindness today!

Good luck!

Random acts of kindness
❀ BINGO

	Help make dinner		Today I ....
Say sorry	Today I	Say hello to three people today	Hold the door for someone
Set the table	Share your		
Make a thank you card for someone	Set the table	Today I	Tell someone you love them

RESOURCEFULNESS

TURNING OBSTACLES INTO OPPORTUNITIES

Turn your **OBSTACLES** into OPPORTUNITIES and your **PROBLEMS** into POSSIBILITIES.

- Roy T. Bennett

When faced with a challenge, it can sometimes seem impossible to overcome. But young people worldwide have repeatedly proven that when you're resourceful, anything is possible!

RESOURCEFULNESS MEANS BEING CREATIVE AND FINDING SOLUTIONS EVEN IN THE TOUGHEST OF SITUATIONS.

It's about recognizing what resources you already have available and making the most of them. It's about getting creative with solutions and being open to new ideas and approaches.

This chapter will explore stories of young people who have accomplished extraordinary things despite limited resources and challenging odds. We will also consider how resourcefulness can help us face difficult obstacles to achieve our goals.

By the end of this chapter, you'll have a greater understanding of why resourcefulness is an important quality to cultivate in order to succeed!

Martha Payne

Martha Payne used her voice to effect change and raised over £140,000 for charity, improving the lives of children around the world.

School lunches — love 'em or hate 'em?!

For most of us, they're a necessary part of the school day. But what if you found out that the food served in your school cafeteria was unhealthy and full of junk food?

This is what happened to nine-year-old Martha Payne from Scotland. The lunches served at her school were so unhealthy that Martha decided to do something about them.

In April 2012, Martha started a blog called NeverSeconds, where she posted photos of the lunches served at her school and reviews of each meal. She rated each lunch out of 10 and gave details of the food and how long it took to eat each meal.

Martha's blog quickly went viral and she started receiving international attention. Her story was featured on the BBC and she even received messages of support from celebrity chef Jamie Oliver.

As a result of Martha's blog, the school lunch menu was improved and healthier food was served. The Scottish government even asked her for advice on improving the meals! In addition, Martha leveraged the visitors to her site to raise over £140,000 (about $175,000) for Mary's Meals. This charity provides school meals to children in poverty-stricken areas.

Martha's story is truly incredible.

SHE USED HER VOICE TO EFFECT CHANGE AND MADE A DIFFERENCE IN THE LIVES OF CHILDREN IN HER OWN COUNTRY AND WORLDWIDE.

Ryan Hickman

AMERICAN ENTREPRENEUR & ENVIRONMENTALIST

Ryan has inspired young people worldwide to take action on environmental issues by showing them that they can make a real difference in protecting our planet.

In the 2008 animated movie "WALL-E," the main character, a little robot, lives in a future world that is one big trash heap. Maybe this was a vision of the future. With plastics and trash polluting our oceans and piling up in our landfills each day, we all have a responsibility to ensure it doesn't become a reality.

Ryan Hickman wants a better future for our planet than the one in "WALL-E." When he was three years old, he and his dad visited a recycling plant. Ryan was amazed at the number of bottles and cans that were being recycled. This inspired Ryan to start walking around his suburb, giving out bags and asking his neighbors to save cans and bottles for him.

But Ryan didn't just want to recycle — he tried to educate people about the importance of reducing waste. His goal was to get people in his community to recycle on a bigger scale. Ryan created his own company, Ryan's Recycling. By the age of seven, his story had gone viral. He had attracted the attention of celebs like Jennifer Aniston and even appeared on the Ellen Degeneres show.

Today, Ryan is a tween, but he has already been recycling for a decade, collecting more than 1.6 million bottles and cans. He serves as the CEO of Ryan's Recycling, which keeps him and his family pretty busy.

While other kids are playing video games or seeing friends, Ryan and his dad drive around his neighborhood in Orange County, California, collecting recycling from the residents. The money he makes from recycling goes into his college fund.

Ryan's recycling has led to a lot of recognition. He has won many awards and accolades, been recognized by Greenpeace for his efforts, and was a finalist for Time magazine's Kid of the Year Award, to name a few of his many achievements.

Through his work, he has been able to inspire others to recycle. He has received messages from as far afield as Dublin and Dubai, from schools that started recycling after following Ryan's examples.

Today, Ryan's Recycling is still going strong. He has also started a new initiative called Project3R–Reduce, Reuse, Recycle, which encourages people to reuse and recycle items.

THE INCREDIBLE WORK OF RYAN AND HIS RECYCLING COMPANY SHOWS HOW, WITH SOME INGENUITY, YOU CAN DEVELOP AN IDEA FOR A BUSINESS THAT BENEFITS YOURSELF AND OTHERS.

He has managed to make money to help pay for his college education while helping the environment at the same time.

Margaret Knight

Margaret Knight's inventive genius revolutionized industrial production in the 19th century, making it safer and more efficient.

Ever wondered who invented the paper bag? Or the machine that ensures your soup is correctly sealed in a can? Well, those inventions, and many more, were created by Margaret Knight.

Born in 1838, Margaret was a gifted inventor and problem solver. As a child, she loved to take things apart and figure out how they worked. Instead of toys, she preferred to play with hammers and nails.

When she was 12, Margaret started working in a textile mill. The textile mills at the time were very dangerous places. There were no safety regulations and accidents happened all the time.

While working at a mill, she witnessed a tragic accident. A worker's hand got caught in a machine and she was severely injured.

The incident inspired Margaret to invent a safety device that stopped machines from operating if someone's hand got caught in them.

Although Margaret made her first invention when she was only young, she invented many more things as an adult. This included the flat-bottomed paper bag (which we still use today) and the machine that manufactures shoes. In all, she held over 30 patents for her inventions.

Margaret's achievements are all the more impressive considering she lived at a time when women were not encouraged to pursue careers in science and engineering. In fact, on many of her patents, she used her initials rather than her full name so that people would not know she was a woman!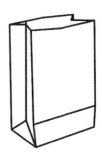

Despite the challenges, Margaret followed her dreams and became one of the most successful inventors of her time.

HER STORY IS ONE OF INSPIRATION AND HOPE, PROVING THAT ANYONE CAN ACHIEVE THEIR DREAMS IF THEY ARE RESOURCEFUL AND DETERMINED.

Kelvin Doe

INVENTOR, DJ & ACTIVIST FROM SIERRA LEONE

Kelvin Doe has inspired a new generation of young inventors and innovators in Sierra Leone and worldwide by demonstrating the potential of human creativity, ingenuity, and determination to make positive change.

Have you ever wanted to be a DJ on your very own radio station?

Imagine being able to broadcast your favorite music and bring important information to your local community.

Kelvin Bokai Doe didn't just imagine it — he did it. He started his radio station using the recycled materials he found around his neighborhood in his home city of Freetown.

Freetown is the capital of Sierra Leone, the West African country where Kelvin grew up as the youngest of five siblings. Sierra Leone was devastated by a civil war in the 1990s, leaving many homeless and without access to health care, water, and electricity.

At only 10, Kelvin started playing around with scrap metal and electronics he found in the trash. He would dismantle the objects he found and put them back together to learn how they worked.

By age 12, Kelvin had taught himself enough engineering skills to build his own batteries by wrapping acid, soda, and metal in tin cups with tape (please do not try this at home!). When there was no electricity in Sierra Leone, Kelvin used his newfound skills to make batteries that gave power to the people in his community.

He even built a generator to help provide his home and others in his neighborhood with electricity when none was available. He would also help his friends by fixing their electronic devices.

At age 15, Kelvin built a radio transmitter, mixer, and microphone. He used these to set up his own community radio station, which broadcasted across his home city of Freetown. Every day, he broadcast under the name DJ Focus, playing music and bringing the people of his community the latest news. "They call me DJ Focus because I believe if you focus, you can do an invention perfectly," he once said. His radio station was powered by the generator he invented himself.

Kelvin entered his homemade radio transmitter into the GMin's Innovate Salone, an innovation challenge for young people from Africa, and won first prize.

In 2012, Kelvin became the youngest person to be invited to the Visiting Practitioner's Program at the Massachusetts Institute of Technology (MIT), which many consider the best technical college in the world. The people at MIT were amazed by Kelvin's inventiveness and a video of his experience traveling to the institute and showing them his inventions went viral.

Those at MIT were not the only ones wowed by Kelvin's abilities. He began to get plenty of attention from people all over the world. He was invited to speak at TEDXTeen and even lectured to undergraduate engineers at Harvard.

He met with world leaders such as Hilary Clinton (US Secretary of State at the time) and Ghana's president Nana Okufo-Addo. Kelvin signed a $100,000 deal with Canadian Internet company Sierra Wi-Fi to create solar-powered solutions. In 2016, he was appointed as an honorary board member of Emergency USA. This charity provides free medical care to people affected by war and poverty.

Today, Kelvin lives and studies in Toronto, Canada, where he hopes to learn skills to return to his country and make a positive difference someday. In 2020, he founded his own start-up, K-Doe Tech, Inc., which sells his electronic inventions. He has also established the Kelvin Doe Foundation, a non-profit organization that supports innovators in finding new ways to uplift their communities.

Kelvin's story is truly incredible. He created devices that improved his community without the luxury of courses or formal education. Instead, he taught himself everything he knew from scratch.

HE IS AN EXCELLENT EXAMPLE OF THE INCREDIBLE ABILITY OF HUMAN BEINGS TO TEACH THEMSELVES NEW SKILLS, COME UP WITH SOLUTIONS, INNOVATE, AND CREATE.

For young kids growing up in Kelvin's home country, he has become a role model and an inspiration. "In Sierra Leone, other young people suddenly feel they can be like Kelvin," said David Sengeh, the country's Minister of Basic and Senior Secondary Education and Chief Innovation Officer.

Kelvin shows that through time, effort, and tenacity, people of any age can teach themselves the skills they need to make a difference in their community. His incredible example has helped inspire a new generation of young inventors and innovators in Sierra Leone and worldwide.

Gitanjali Rao

AMERICAN SCIENTIST, INVENTOR, ACTIVIST & AUTHOR

Gitanjali Rao has developed groundbreaking inventions to help detect and prevent water contamination, cyberbullying, and cancer. Her work has impacted countless lives world-wide, making her one of the most influential young people in the world today.

What comes to mind when you think of a famous, award-winning inventor?

For most of us, the image that pops into our heads is probably an adult in a white lab coat. But the truth is anyone can be an inventor — no matter how young or old. Gitanjali Rao is living proof of this. She has been inventing things that help improve the world since she was 10.

Today, at 16 years old, in addition to her work as an inventor, the US teenager is also a scientist, engineer, social activist, and author. Not a bad resumé for someone who has not yet completed high school!

Gitanjali began her inventing journey in 2015 after hearing about the water crisis in the city of Flint, Michigan. The city had switched from getting its water from the Detroit water system to the Flint River, which was contaminated with lead and a dangerous bacteria called Legionella. She was shocked to learn that people were getting sick from the water they were drinking, and she wanted to do something to help.

She soon realized that lead contamination is a problem in many cities around the world, not just Flint. In places such as India, lead contamination in water is a major issue that results in lead poisoning.

But testing water is expensive and time-consuming. So, Gitanjali invented a device called Tethys that uses carbon nanotubes to test for lead in water. It's affordable, fast, and easy to use.

In 2017, when Gitanjali was 12 years old, she won $25,000 to help develop her invention. A year later, she presented the device at the annual MAKERS conference and raised another $25,000. In 2019, she began working with the Denver water facility to create a Tethys prototype.

Today, she is waiting for a patent on her product so she can market and sell it and help people around the world avoid drinking contaminated water.

But Gitanjali didn't stop there. She found time to develop Kindly, an app that detects and stops cyberbullying, in partnership with the United Nations Children's Fund (UNICEF).

She also developed a diagnostic tool called Epione that uses genetic information to detect addiction to a type of painkiller called opioids, which can be extremely dangerous for those who become dependent on them.

When she's not coming up with new inventions, Gitanjali is devoted to promoting STEM subjects at schools. She wrote the book "Young Inventor's Guide to STEM," which has been translated into five languages. The book details her five-step problem-solving technique for learners, teachers, and parents.

She has also reached more than 70,000 young people worldwide through her STEM-based innovation workshops, which aim to inspire a new generation of inventors, engineers, scientists, developers, and mathematicians. She has spoken over 200 times about STEM, not just in her home country of the United States but also in Western Africa, the Middle East, Asia, South America, Europe, Canada, and Australia.

Gitanjali's fantastic ability to invent game-changing new technology and her dedication to sharing her knowledge with others has led to fame, recognition, and many awards and accolades.

In 2020, she made the cover of Time magazine when she became the first to win the publication's new Kid of the Year Award. She has also spoken at TEDx four times and won the

United States Environmental Protection Agency President's Environmental Youth Award in 2018.

Gitanjali is driven not by a desire for fame or fortune, but by her genuine passion for spreading the role that STEM can play in lifting young people out of poverty. She has served as a mentor to young people in refugee camps in places such as Kenya and Cambodia, as well as kids in rural areas of the US. Her aim? To get more young people involved in science and technology.

Gitanjali is a living example of how young people can significantly impact the world.

HER INTELLECTUAL CURIOSITY AND DESIRE TO HELP PEOPLE THROUGH HER INVENTIONS EXEMPLIFY THE HUMAN SPIRIT AT ITS MOST INGENIOUS.

She has inspired thousands of young kids to invent and innovate. We hope that, through reading about her story, she has been able to inspire you, too.

Louis Braille

FRENCH EDUCATOR AND INVENTOR

Louis Braille's system of raised dots revolutionized literacy for blind people, empowering them to be more independent.

Being able to see is something that many of us take for granted. We wake up in the morning, open our eyes, and see the world around us. But for some people, this isn't possible. They are blind, which means that they can't see at all.

One of the most famous blind people in history is Louis Braille. He was born in France in 1809. When he was three years old, he had an accident that injured his eye. Unfortunately, the injury got infected. By the time Louis was five years old, he was completely blind.

At that time, there were no schools for blind children in France, so Louis's father placed him in an institute for the blind run by a man named Valentin Haüy.

Haüy believed that all people, no matter their disability, deserved to be educated. He developed a system of raised letters that blind people could feel with their fingers so they could learn to read. However, this system was complicated and took a long time to learn.

Louis Braille was a bright student and quickly learned Haüy's system of raised letters, but he wanted to find a better way for blind people to read and write.

As a 12-year-old blind student, Louis spent hours trying to develop a better system — and finally, he did. When he was 15, he completed a code of raised dots that could be read quickly and easily by touching them with his fingers. This system was much easier to use than Haüy's system of raised letters, and it didn't take as long to learn. Braille called his method "braille."

But only some people were convinced that Braille's system was better. While Louis taught it to some of his fellow students and later his pupils when he began to teach at the institute, it wasn't widely adopted.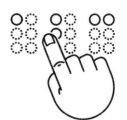

It wasn't until after Louis Braille's premature death in 1852 that his system became widely used.

Now, over 150 years later, braille is used all over the world by people who are blind or have low vision. It has allowed them to attend school, get jobs, and live more independently. It has even been adapted to work with computers.

AND IT ALL STARTED WITH ONE YOUNG BOY'S

DETERMINATION TO FIND A BETTER WAY.

Activity - Over to YOU!

We have met some incredible young people who have inspired us with their courage, creativity, determination, optimism, compassion, and resourcefulness. Now it's your turn to write your story.

Think about what makes you unique and how you want to make your mark on the world. It could be anything from making a difference in your local community to starting an online business. It could be recycling, playing an instrument, or helping the homeless.

Now imagine you can jump 10 years into the future. What would you have accomplished and what impact would you have made? How did you make a difference in the world and achieve your goals?

Take some time to write down all the details of your story. Describe how it felt, who helped you along the way, and any challenges you faced.

Finally, take a step back and reflect on your story. What were the keys to success for you? How did courage, creativity, determination, optimism, compassion, and resourcefulness help you achieve your goals?

Good luck writing your story.

Remember that anything is possible if you believe in yourself! With a bit of hard work and dedication, you can be the hero of your own story.

Now it's your turn... draw your portrait:

Your Name:

. . . .

. . . .

Date of Birth

. . . .

. . . .

What will you be remembered for?

. . . .

. . . .

What's your favorite quote? Write it down here:

Write your story:

CONCLUSION

INSPIRING A NEW GENERATION
OF CHANGE MAKERS

EVERYONE

you ADMIRE

Was once a

BEGINNER.

- Jack Butcher

This book has presented the stories of incredible young people who have achieved remarkable feats. From climbing mountains to starting charities, these amazing kids have shown us what it takes to make a difference in the world.

You might be thinking, "How can I make a difference? I am just one person." But these incredible kids have shown us that anyone can make a difference.

Remember, all the successful people today started from the bottom.

THEY ARE NOT SUPERHUMAN. THEY ARE JUST ORDINARY KIDS WITH BIG DREAMS. THEY HAVE GOOD DAYS, BAD DAYS, SUCCESSES, AND FAILURES, BUT THEY KEEP GOING, BELIEVE IN THEMSELVES, AND NEVER GIVE UP.

Take inspiration from these remarkable young people. Find your passion. What are you into? What do you love? What makes you come alive? Whatever it is, follow it. Start small, work towards the future you want to see, and never give up on your dreams.

You have the power to change the world. Believe in yourself and start now.

Good luck!

TAKING ACTION

YOU CAN MAKE A DIFFERENCE

THE FUTURE

belongs to those

who *BELIEVE* in

the *BEAUTY*

of THEIR DREAMS.

- Eleanor Roosevelt

Hopefully you've been inspired to take action and make your own mark on the world. There are many ways to get involved and make a difference, regardless of age.

Here are some of our top tips:

- **Start small** — Explore your passions and figure out how to make a difference. It doesn't have to be big. You could start a club at school with friends to learn about an issue or work on a project you're passionate about. Remember, even small acts of kindness or activism can have a significant impact.
- **Start a fundraiser** — Use platforms like GoFundMe or JustGiving to help fundraise for causes you believe in. You can also team up with friends and family to make a bigger impact.
- **Get involved** — Talk to your family, teachers, or other adults. Read and learn more about the issues that you care about. Find out what others in your community are doing and see if there's something you can help with. Find an organization that works on an issue you are passionate about and volunteer or fundraise for it.
- **Speak out** — Use your voice and share your message with the world. If you know something isn't right, stand up for what you believe in. Spread awareness and be an advocate for the causes you care about. Organize a community event or gathering to bring attention to an issue. Keep a blog or social media page to discuss your concerns.

- **Have fun** — Don't forget to have fun and be creative. Whether through art, music, dance, or whatever you enjoy, stay true to who you are and have a good time!
- **Believe in yourself** — You have the power to make a difference!

Whatever you do, wherever you go, whatever you believe in — never forget that you can make a difference. Remember these fantastic young people who have achieved incredible things and use them as inspiration. And finally, don't forget — everything starts with a small step.

THE SKY IS THE LIMIT! GOOD LUCK, AND NEVER GIVE UP ON YOUR DREAMS!

THANKS
FOR READING OUR
BOOK!

We really hope that you and your child are inspired by the incredible women featured in this book.

We would be so grateful if you could take a few seconds to leave an honest review or a star rating on Amazon. (A star rating takes just a couple of clicks).

Your review also helps other parents discover this book, and it might help their tween children on their journeys. Plus, it will also be good Karma for you.

To leave a review

LIKED THIS BOOK?
WE THINK YOU'LL
LOVE THESE!

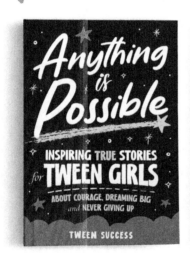 

Get your copy
SCAN
HERE

Printed in Great Britain
by Amazon

33745858R00086